ABOUT BOOK

A romance story about a young, clumsy nurse who struggles through thick and thin to be with her prince charming. In the quest of finding her prince charming she is faced with a lot of challenges which life throws at her. Would she be able to face these challenges? If you want to follow her on this her interesting and epic journey you better grab a copy of this interesting romance series and also don't forget to bring along your bucket of pop corn.

CLUMSY_NURSE

Chapter two

CYNTHIA'S POV

Am on my bed, Diana is already gone I had already chosen my outfit for the heath conference I heard Randy is going to be there who knows I might meet him I want to ask my mother about the lady In the beautiful room but am scared she might find out I went there .So let me introduce myself a little My name is Cynthia David, My mother is a nurse in (A. G. H. C)But for now she is resting because she lied that her leg is hurting, but I think she just grew lazy of work She normally does this and whenever we become broke she rushes back to work, my mum is really funny I am 21 I will be 22 Soon but you won't believe it, I don't have a boyfriend and most annoyingly am still a virgin, even Diana is not a virgin anyways am waiting for my Mr. right. I might be clumsy but I don't think any nurse in A. G. H. C is more brilliant than i am because I was a nurse right from when I was born. my mom thought me so much I am fair but not white, I have long pretty hair, my figure is quite attractive I think nature didn't cheat on me when it comes to appearance, My father has a supermarket I go there every now and then Am the only child but I have an elder sister she is not actually my mother's daughter but she is my sweet cousin "lia" she traveled and i miss her, Ok that's enough of me.

Back to present

i wanted to go to the living room and ask my mom about the 3rd floor but she just walked into my room with my food, I collected the plate from her and she sat on the bed Right now my mother is touching my hair in that manner, this means she wants to ask the same question again, the same annoying question……"Cynthia have you later gotten a boyfriend", she asked "Mom!!!!" I scream "Sorry, Sorry I was just asking "She said***I Will use this opportunity to ask her ***"Mom the lady in the 3rd floor, "who is she?"What!! Cynthia when did you Go there, "do you want sir Grande to kill you, "do you want to get killed, "how did you even enter?"What about the guards "?She asked all this at once, I scratched my hair "Mom I didn't go there live, I was in my dream like this……I lay down and closed my eye then I opened them and continued "In my dream mom i heard the voice of God, he said "come my daughter ""Really my child, she asked I sat up "Yes mom and he took me to that room spiritually and I saw the pretty lady there, mum she was so beautiful, My mom got interested "What else did God say? ", she asked "He said go home and ask your mother what is happening in the third floor "Really",? She asked "Yes mom and he said, tell Mrs. David to say the truth if not the punishment of heaven will fall on her" i said with a scared face. Really? , come I will tell you all I know" She said I sat up in interest grinning like a fried dried goat."Her name is Anita Grande she is the first and most loved daughter of sir Alexander Grande the owner and founder of(A. G. H C)"Ohhh is that so""Yes she is in coma because she had an accident, do you know Randy?"No mom, but I have heard about him."Randy did everything humanly possible to wake Anita up, He operated on her almost every day after the accident and it was confirmed that Anita was okay but no one knows why she Is not waking up."She Is the only patient Randy treated that didn't wake up."But mom who so she to him ", i asked."Well the two hospitals where in competition so they decided to become one by getting their children married,"Omg mom, "Is Randy married ""No my child but he was engaged to marry Anita, as we heard at first she didn't love him neither did he love her but with Time their love became strong."Mmmmmmm awesome" i replied smiling "Anita was a goddess, she was very intelligent and did her duties well she had such a powerful aura that when she passed by her presence was felt everywhere."Wow she was great ", i replied."But mom what about her family."The third floor looks so beautiful because Mr. Grande didn't want to believe that his only jewel is in coma so he designed her coma into a very beautiful room."He also assigned a maid who always dressed her up and made her look pretty everyday... while we await her wake up "No wonder her comma is so attractive, i replied."Yes that's why it is" she answered "But, what about her mother."Actually her mother is missing, after Anita's accident she was seen no more and her father does not come out anymore nobody knows what's wrong."His other wife Mrs. Tonia Grande is now in charge of the company" she replied..."Oh the grumpy woman Daniela mom right?, I asked."Yes my child ", she replied" I wish Anita will stand up" i said."Me too my child" she replied. She carried up the pretty gown on my bed "My child is this outfit for the conference? She asked "Yes mom it is ", i replied "It's pretty I wish you will meet some rich boy and get a boyfriend", she replied"Ohhhhh mom " i said frowning my face "Sorry, sorry you are free to die a virgin I won't disturb you anymore " she replied as she placed the food on my lap and walked out Argh, i placed my hands under my jaw, what a painful story I just heard***Oh Randy my mystery crush why are you engaged to my Bestie this is what the call unrequited attraction *** i Said to myself

RANDY'S POV

Am waiting for my doctor to come out she is the one that operated me about the hole in my heart; i sat quietly waiting for her until she walked out."Oh Randy welcome", she said "Doctor how are you "Am fine but, how is your heart?"That's why I came; you said I will be fine after the surgery."I also said you should drink your routine drugs for 2 months didn't i."But this is already one month and I still receive signs when I don't drink them."Randy the surgery did its part, now the drugs will do its part. So am sure that after two months all signs and signals will seize."I hope so too ", i replied her. I stood up and walked to the door my guards followed me to my car I entered the second car while they followed the first car.

SIR ALEXANDER GRANDE POV

I am lying still on the bed, I was just a little sick but after this doctor started treatment I feel like am dying, I can't even move anymore and I want to see my Anita. The doctor is injecting me right now, I want to ask him questions but speaking is now difficult for me "Sir Alexandra Grande you will feel better after this treatment. I slowly nodded to him and he walked out just then I sat up and the Maid walked in with my morning coffee I don't know why but nowadays I think this coffee is making me weak.

"No DONT worry just get me water I replied her"Ok sir, she said and walked out just then

Tonia walked in with the same cup of tea "My love please take your coffee please" she said "No I don't want it ", i replied"Ok your wish" she replied as she walked out of the room I lay back on my bed I really miss Anita and her mother Ciara..

RANDY'S POV

I arrived home; I actually have a house here where I live alone. I dropped my bag on the couch and the Maids took it upstairs I removed my suite and handed it over to the other maid the room is a little dim but am used to it so I can still find my way. I walked to Anita's picture in my glass closet and looked at it i switch on the closet light so i can see her very well sparkling in that white glass. My maid called on me so I turned "How may I help", I asked, Sir someone is here for you she replied "Let them in, i replied. I switch on the light because I have visitor but normally I stay with the lights dim or off. I like my environment to match my mood and this darkness matched the darkness in my heart...

DANIELA'S POV

I heard Randy is back I drove directly to his house, our former love garden. I walk into the room there he is but first i see is Anita's picture inside the glass closet that sparkled white light "Randy it's been long" i Said."Daniela how have you been" he said this as he walked to his table and took his bottle water which he held in his hands and walked outside to the pool where he stood facing the water. I met Randy In Paris we fell in love and we were dating at that time Anita was the talk of the whole family but Randy was all I wanted I didn't even care about shares or (A. G. H. C)Until i wake up one morning and hear that the heir of(A. G. H. C) is betrothed to the heir of (dervantes health world)What is going on, I asked myself why is my Randy betrothed to Anita, why must Anita take everything away from me. Randy told me he didn't love Anita that it was just formalities, I know he was betrothed to Anita but his body and love was still mine and mine alone Until one day Randy told me that he had fallen in love with Anita and he wanted to spend the rest of his life with her, he told me to stay out of his life for good Just like that, like an old movie, like a used sachet lying on the road, Randy forgot me.

BACK TO PRESENT

I rushed after Randy and took his hands"Randy Anita is gone don't you get it, you guys were never meant to be, this is our signal to start our love afresh, it's still me you love me so much remember. I turn his face to look at me but all I see is tears filled in his pretty, sexy eye."Daniela go" am not in the mood to talk, he replied, He tried walking out but I ran over to his face

"Daniela am not in the.......I didn't let him talk anymore I just kissed him Randy slowly pushed me away "Daniela that's enough, you need to leave. He said and before I could talk he dragged me to my car and when I sat down he gave his driver signals to take me home and before I could say Jack and John I was already on the street to my home.

RANDY'S POV

Finally Daniela is gone, the love and attention Daniela wants now is something that will never happen. I tried lying back when my assistant called my line**Mmmm seems like she finally decided to travel down ***I picked up the call “Tell me Iren, what is it” . I asked “Actually sir, I just came from the meeting concerning the conference “, she replied “Tell me what was concluded “? , i asked “Because your safety is important they decided you will go as a commoner and you will Dress casual the people will only know who you are when you are called on stage sir ”What’s the point? I asked “It’s for your safety sir, people don’t know you very well yet and that’s good for us you will now be introduced once and for all.Ok fine i understand... I replied “That will be all sir” Iren replied. I dropped the call. Actually I like this concept better; I don’t even have strength for the press or the crowd pursuing me. I walked down and picked my guitar which stood across the wall sat quietly and played a steady painful tune, music is the only sound that makes me feel better and am quite good at it..

Mrs. TONIA POV (Anita's step-mom)

What is going on with Grande if he keeps rejecting this tea how I kill him off, Well I better take a break before he finds out, I sat on my bed I was so deep in thought, I need to stop being Anita's cover am just playing her role and I have no actual shares how long will this continue, I tried lying back but i heard sobbing in the passage so I opened the door to my room just to see my precious daughter sitting on the floor crying "Daniela, what's wrong with you Mom Anita is dead, Anita is gone, there is no hope right? , so why can't Randy love me. "It's been two years, it's been two fucking years, why is it so hard for Randy to move on mom? She said crying...

"It's all right Daniela Randy has a lot on his mind for now so just let him cool down, i replied. I dragged her up into my room and she sat on the bed beside me...

CYNTHIA'S POV

I have already arranged everything for the conference tomorrow, I am so happy. I open my window and I feel this heavy breeze, the weather feels really cold it might be cold tomorrow I better change my outfit I returned the outfit into the box and brought out something else I am sure this will match my generation bag, I Carefully placed the red bag on the bed because my generation bag can't touch the floor, I combed my hair in the mirror and played my hip pop music which helps me sleep well and soundly hours later, It's morning my stupid alarm started again so I pushed it down and continued my sleep minutes later, What's going on who is dragging my leg I opened my eye it's my mother "Cynthia the conference is about starting ", She said "Omg mom, I over slept."Hurry go and bath, she said.

"Ok mother "I rushed into the shower were I took a quick and very quick bath...

RANDY'S POV

Totally unlike me i woke really late. I rushed into the shower first minutes later I rushed down and had breakfast, my guards were already dressed in a casual outfit the waited outside while I enjoyed my meal****Today is going to be so stressful God help me ****

CNTHIA'S POV

Am already dressed up and ready. I ran into the dinner to have breakfast I Carefully placed my generation bag on the dining table.I don't know why but my mother and father are laughing at my outfit, anyways I don't Care. I hurriedly took a chicken Lap and placed it on my rice Mom, dad, good morning I said "Thanks dear ", my dad replied"Oh finally you remember us", my mom said.I was busy with my food I didn't even reply."Cynthia didn't you see something else to wear I mean it's not snowing" my dad said."Dad!!! Don't disturb my meal", i said. "Sorry, eat up ", he said. I know my mom is still laughing slowly, although she hides her face when I look at her I still know what she's doing. I hurried my meal minutes later, am already running down the streets my phone is ringing I instantly pick up and its Diana "Cynthia are you there." no but........ I was caught up in the call i didn't see myself hitting a rock, i slipped and fell flat on the ground Ouch that hurt, but my hands are high up am making sure my generation bag doesn't touch the ground...

•••

I pull myself up and continue the call while limping "Diana where are you?, I asked" Cynthia am going to be delayed so save a seat for me near the stair."Ok i will ", i replied. Personally i also like sitting near the stair during conferences it makes it easy to sneak out.I walked to the street junction; I took a cab and headed for the program. Minutes later just arrived the conference hall.I sighted the roll of sits near the stair case, I rushed to the first line this way I will watch the speaker well. The place was getting crowded bit by bit.I saw a man selling handouts in his wheelbarrow, who knows if he will have Handbook on how to be a proper nurse. I placed my red bag on the chair I was planning on sitting, while I placed my book on the chair I kept for Cynthia. I ran after the handout man but he was stupidly moving fast"Hey!! Hey!!! Handout". I shouted. Although the heaviness of my outfit didn't let me run well....Oh finally he stopped, I took the handout that caught my eye the title was "Act like a lady "I stood In front of his truck and I went through my book, the conference hall kept filing up but I already got a seat so I don't care. I was there reading the book, he doesn't know but i have plans of finishing this small book and returning it to this man because I don't even have money with me..

•••

Someone is covering my eye from behind, I know it's Diana her perfume exposed her."Diana, I know it's you" I said and She laughed as she removed her hands she took the other book on the man's shore a lot of people read from the man's barrow. Diana turned her book and said the title out loud."Hand out on how to make sex more fun", Cynthia I think you need this ". She said.****Is she crazy******"Hey are you ok, I have not even had sex and you talk of making it fun", I shouted. Everybody turned to look at me Omg; i got embarrassed I tried changing my statement "Actually I mean, I have not had sex this week, this week that's what I meant. So face your business stop looking at me huh.All of them turned to their business

Diana smiled at me i took the sex book from her I wanted to look through it."Cynthia the hall is getting filled up", Diana shouted."Yes it is ", i replied while reading my sex book with interest.

RANDY'S POV

I just arrived at the conference everywhere is already filled up.I look casual enough I guess and my guards are also looking casual.“Sir I think the first chair close to the stair is the best choice “, one guard said“Ok let’s go “, I replied him We arrived at the first roll close to the stairs and only 3 seats were empty when i looked first i think I saw a red bag on one seat but when I finally looked down well it was on the floor. Is my sight disturbing or did my guards drop it.I sat on the empty chair since the other chair had a book on it.“Guys did you drop a lady’s bag on the floor “, i asked them“No, it was on the floor when we arrived “, a guard replied.“Ok “, i replied as I dropped my phone in the empty chair.**I just can’t wait for the conference to start **

DIANA’S POV

I saw the guy sitting on Cynthia's section.I know this guy looks like Randy because I have been close to Randy before."I was one of the nurses in the room when he operated on Anita. I tapped Cynthia and she turned to look at her seat "Hey, who is that "? She asked me"I don't know but........Before i could finish Cynthia already ran off, she ran straight to where the strikingly cute guy sat.I tried running after her but I just realized she ran off with the books so I opened my purse to pay the bookseller. The environment was so calm no one spoke anymore the conference had already started. I paid him and i collected my change. I climbed the stairs back up, I did this slowly because everywhere was so quiet I didn't want to be noticed.Just then I heard Cynthia's voice scream ...."Hey! How dare you drop my generation bag on the floor? She yelled.

Everybody in the hall turned to look at her***Omg whenever Cynthia screams like this the person she screamed at is in trouble***I rush up to her as fast as i can and that was when I confirmed, it was really

"Randy devantes"." what the fuck!!!!! , hey, Who is this crazy woman? ", Randy asked his guards with a confused and frustrated face ,"What crazy woman, me crazy woman, hey!!! Do you want to die?, Cynthia screamed again Randy flipped his hair backward as he looked around in embarrassment.

"Please can you just take this crazy woman out of here huh?" please just take her out!!! , He ordered while looking at his guards.

**Wow i must say, these two seem to be a perfect match of crazy.I said to myself...

•••

Randy's guards turned to Cynthia

"Madam please you need to leave you are creating a scene" they said "What!!! Cynthia exclaimed in disbelief She bent down and picked the bag next thing she started talking to the bag"Oh my generation bag don't mind this guy here, this stupid guy. Randy looked In her face "Hey! He shunned, next thing Cynthia tried to slap him but she withdrew her hands" If not for one thing I will just slap you here, She said smirking and pointing at him. Randy was so frustrated and his guards where not helping matters they were lost looking at Cynthia. They had not seen a thing like this in there live "Arrrgh, I should have known today was a bad day. Why can't you just drag this stupid girl away from here? He yelled angrily at his guards."We are sorry sir, hey woman they tried dragging Cynthia out but she pushed them away. Cynthia Pointed the bag to Randy's face "Hey I am watching you, better watch you back. She said to him with a serious face Randy looked scared.

I have been trying to give Cynthia signals since that this person was Randy devantes but she isn't paying attention to me, so I gave her the signals that this person deserves respect and that the person can fire her and finally she got it, but it was already too late as four men in suite just arrived..

•••

CYNTHIA'S POV

Oh am finished so this person is someone that deserves respect. Why didn't Diana signal me earlier, Omg what do I do.I looked at Randy's frustrated face and I knew I was in for it, The men In suite arrived"Do you know who you are troubling young lady, "One of them asked me "What are you doing let's take her to jail, the other said"Sorry for the inconveniences sir, the other said to the cute guy I just fought with.Am still in shock, why are they calling this small boy sir, I felt like slapping him, my anger was written all over my face even my teeth's were out .He looked at my face and I smiled by force while bowing to him, Am finished today, I hope he forgives me 'Going to prison is not enough, this woman is just crazy and reckless she even threatened to kill me ", he said to the men."But why do you drop my generation bag on the floor are you stupid? .... just then I saw Diana giving me signals that (am dead). So I finished the statement with "sir ".I sounded more like," why do you drop my generation bag on the floor are you stupid... sir ".The cute guy almost went crazy, he looked around in frustration and embarrassment.

•••

“What, am I stupid sir? “Am I stupid sir? “, imagine that polite insult. Just arrest this this girl already, he ordered in frustration. I instantly bowed to him In such a way that my hair covered my face, Diana signaled me that he deserves respect, I don’t know if he is a Prince, or a king, or a majesty, or a president. Oh am so confused“Sir, my king, your honor, your majesty. Am sorry huh? .... the thing is, insanity runs in my family, don’t mind me, I tried touching his shoes but he ran away scared, I almost laughed.“Hey!Don’t touch me, Are you a nurse,He asked me.Yes I am .... I saw Diana signals again so i quickly changed my statement, no am not. I said.He turned to the men on suite “its okay, prison is too extreme, find out the hospital she works for and fire her as Soon as possible"Hey!!! , I yelled losing my cool" Who do you……. I saw Diana's face so I changed my statement instantly.. … Who do you love sir, do you love God? I asked him.He looked at me from hair to toe"I wonder which crazy hospital have youas a nurse; you don't have patience is this how you treat patients? Tell me your hospital so I can inform them on how to treat clumsy nurses". He replied while dialing his phone"Huh, tell me. He said raising his brows, I instantly bent down and picked the biscuits sachet a child just dropped"Sir, your majesty, you are getting it wrong, am not a Nurse, I am the assistant cleaner. I am busy doing my job of picking stuffs on the floor. I said.The men in suite looked at me,

***Am dead ***

I slowly picked up all the sachets on the floor until i got a little bit far from them.I ran away as fast as I could and Diana ran after me.She took some of the sachets from me and we threw into the dust bin. We ran away until we ran into the Matron who was walking in."Cynthia, Diana, were to? Come on, let's go to the conference. She said

***Con what, conference. Hah, I can't go back there and Matron Linda might drag me there, and that guy will find out am a nurse in (A. G. H. C) and he will fire me. ***Omg what to do, I scratched my head in confusion."Come on girls lets go back".She walked in front, Diana walked behind her "Matron the thing is I can't go with you" i said."Why Cynthia? She asked me."Well my dad just passed out RIGHT now at his shop."Omg that's bad, why did he faint?"Well I heard it was the velocity of the lie a customer told."Then it's just a joke, come on.No, he's blood pressure is 1000 right now."Omg Cynthia go home pls."Yes I am Going" I replied as I Bowed, I lifted my face and my eye met with that of the cute guy I fought with I instantly sticked out my tongue, he formed a mouth as though he wanted to insult me.I instantly waved at Diana and ran home as fast as I could...

•••

Wow thank God I didn't go back there; I would have just lost my job.I wonder who that guys is, because of him I just missed my conference, I missed my only opportunity to meet Randy, Well no problem , I better head home right away.

RANDY'S POV

Wow am Glad that girl left, now everyone is looking at me.What Kind of girl is that She was dressed like a mango treeShe was talking to a bagAnd the book she was reading"How to make sex fun"Omg how can a decent girl read such book in public. Wow i have met a CLUMSY Person today. I sat down thinking to myself when the speaker called my name so I stood up. Everyone was shocked I was so embarrassed that I had to wear my glasses; I walked up to the stage and took the Mic, My guards stood behind me.

CYNTHIA'S POV

Wow its 7 pm the conference must have been over by now.I can't believe I slept for 6 hours,I need to call Diana so she can tell me how the conference wentI picked my phone from my cupboardOmg my batteries are out what will I do this is bad, how will I call Diana.Well tomorrow is still another day...

DIANA'S POV

Wow i can't wait to tell Cynthia that the Person she fought with was RandyI need to call her right away

I tried calling Cynthia but her phone was switched off.Wow this is bad.I lay in my bed when my phone rang so I picked up the call, it was Juliet one of the senior nurses in my rank."Hey July ", i said"I have been trying to call Cynthia, we just received news that the nurse who will accompany sir Randy will be chosen from(A. G. H. C)"Wow that's nice ", i replied, "Yes and sir Randy said he doesn't want a dummy so he set the exam questions himself. And the exam is tomorrow on the

10th floor, Omg I am not prepared and neither is Cynthia her phone is off again. Anyways thank you.I dropped the call.** Wow staying in the same house with Randy devantes that's every girls dream **I can't wait to inform CynthiaI was about walking into the shower when my phone rang again it Tony. Omg I forgot to inform Cynthia I set her up on a blind date with Doctor Tony from R. D hospitals. He is young and handsome just like Randy; he is a friend of my boyfriend Ethan. I and Ethan planned this, I feel so bad that Cynthia doesn't have a boyfriend it's so annoying. I picked his call. Hello good day"Hey Diana, eehhm the girl you and Ethan talked about is she meeting, Well I have not spoken to Cynthia yet but she will come out for sure that's certain"Ok I look forward to meeting her I have heard a lot about her already, Ok no problem..

TONY'S POV

I have earned everything I need for a good life, I have solved all the puzzles of life, the only puzzle I can't solve is women. Am the second best doctor in R. D. Hospitals, I base in Paris I just came back 6 months before and Ethan is my best friend right from high school although he is a lab technician not a doctor, I have seen pictures of this Cynthia girl on his phone, The fact that she is playful attracts me most to her, I look forward to meeting you Cynthia..

TO BE CONTINUED…………..

www.ingramcontent.com/pod-product-compliance
Lightning Source LLC
LaVergne TN
LVHW052111160826
845678LV00015B/3496
* 9 7 9 8 8 4 4 3 6 8 2 1 9 *